Englisch-Stars
4

Comics

Erarbeitet von

Barbara Gleich
Irene Reindl
Katrin Schmidt
Britta Schöpe

Comic

Olivia's holidays

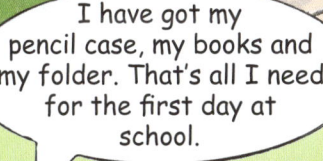

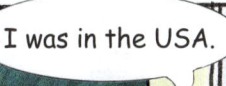

1. Find the words. Circle them and draw lines.

pencilschoolbagfolderbookpenscissorsrubberpencilcaseruler

2. Trace the lines and write.

John   Gloria   Marty   Sophie

Finde heraus, wo die Kinder ihre Ferien verbracht haben.

John spent his holidays in the _____.

Gloria spent her holidays at the _____.

Marty spent his holidays in the _____.

Sophie spent her holidays in _____.

| USA |
| beach |
| mountains |
| Scotland |

3. Match the sentences with the correct picture.

Ordne die Sätze den Bildern zu, indem du die richtige Zahl in die Kreise schreibst.

There are pencils, a pen, a ruler, a rubber and a pair of scissors in my pencil case.

Mary was such a nice girl. I will write an e-mail to her.

Okay, Dad. But look at the wonderful seashells I found at the beach.

I have got my pencil case, my books and my folder.

Welche Aussagen stimmen und welche sind falsch? Die richtigen Antworten ergeben zusammengesetzt das Lösungswort.

4. Correct or wrong? Find out what Sally says.

I love _____.

	correct	wrong
Olivia found seashells at the beach.	ho	we
Olivia's new friend is called Maisy.	ek	li
There's a stick of glue in Olivia's pencil case.	en	da
Olivia has got a pencil case, books and a folder in her schoolbag.	ys	ds

📕 Comic

Numbers in the night

..., seven, eight, ...

..., ten, eleven, ...

..., thirteen, ...

Who's counting there?
It must be Koala.

Is he counting his
toys? Wow, he has
got a lot of toys ...

..., seventeen, ...

..., thirty, ...

Or is he counting
lollipops? Oh, that's
fantastic, so many
lollipops!

Or is he counting
money? Wow, Koala
is really rich.

..., seventy, ...

I can't sleep.
I'm counting sheep
to get tired.

Oh!

What are you
counting?

1. Count and write.

Zähle und schreibe als Wort und Zahl.

卌 卌 III _____ ◯   卌 卌 卌 IIII _____ ◯

卌 卌 卌 _____ ◯   卌 卌 II _____ ◯

卌 卌 卌 II _____ ◯   卌 卌 卌 卌 _____ ◯

卌 卌 I _____ ◯   卌 卌 IIII _____ ◯

卌 卌 卌 I _____ ◯   卌 卌 卌 III _____ ◯

> **eleven twelve thirteen fourteen fifteen sixteen
> seventeen eighteen nineteen twenty**

2. Colour.

ten + twenty = green   twenty + thirty = brown

thirty + fifty = yellow   fifty + forty = red

ninety – thirty = blue   sixty – twenty = pink

fifty – thirty = grey   one hundred – thirty = orange

Löse zuerst die Rechenaufgaben und male dann in der richtigen Farbe an.

3. Correct or wrong? Find the correct number and write.

> Rechne jeweils die Aufgabe der richtigen Antwort aus. Schaue in der Tabelle nach, welcher Buchstabe zu dem Ergebnis gehört. Die Buchstaben aller richtigen Antworten ergeben die Lösung.

	correct	wrong
Sally is Koala's friend.	10 + 80	20 + 80
Koala is sleeping.	30 + 40	40 + 60
Sally wakes up.	20 + 80	70 − 10
Koala has got many toys.	90 − 60	80 − 40
Sally is counting lollipops.	15 + 15	20 + 30
Koala is counting.	50 + 50	10 + 10
Koala can't sleep.	20 − 10	30 − 10

____ ___!

ten = B	sixty = E
twenty = I	seventy = H
thirty = C	eighty = F
fourty = D	ninety = G
fifty = J	one hundred = O

 Comic

New furniture for Ben

✏️ 1. What's wrong? Complete the sentences.

> Schau genau hin. Nicht alle Möbelstücke sind an ihrem richtigen Platz. Vervollständige die Sätze.

There's a  _____ lamp _____ in the _____ bathroom _____ .

There's a _____ in the _____ .

There's a _____ in the _____ .

There's a _____ in the _____ .

There's a _____ in the _____ .

There's a _____ in the _____ .

There's a _____ on the _____ .

There are _____ in the _____ .

**living room bedroom kitchen garden garage toilet stairs
bathroom lamp table bed sofa cupboard shelves desk chair**

2. Complete the sentences. Draw lines.

The shelves are   for the living room.

The cupboards are   too big.

The sofa is   for the kitchen.

The armchair is   for the bathroom.

3. Complete the sentences and number.

1   2   3   4

○ I'd love to do my homework in this _____. It's so comfortable.

○ Look at this fantastic _____.

○ These _____ are great. I'll have enough room to play on the floor.

○ Mum, look at these _____. They are really nice.

11

📕 Comic

Jenny is hungry

1. What do they like? Read, write and draw.

Verbinde die Sprech-
blasen jeweils mit dem
richtigen Teller und zeichne
dazu was fehlt. Fahre die
grauen Wörter nach.

I like sausage
with mashed
potatoes.

I like cheese
salad with
bread.

I like fish and
chips.

I like tomato
soup and a
roll.

I like strawberry
ice-cream and chocolate
ice-cream.

2. Do the crossword.

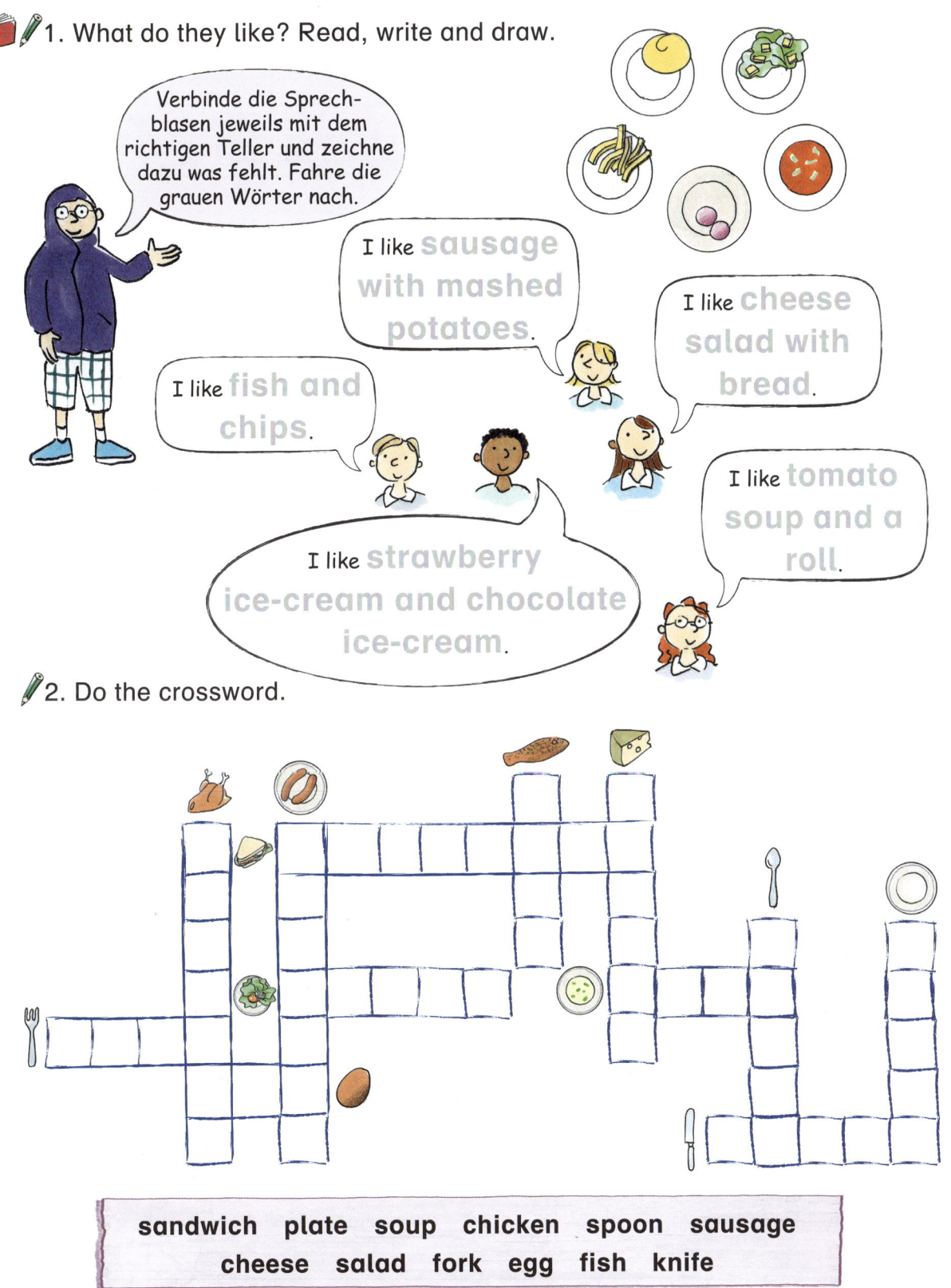

sandwich   plate   soup   chicken   spoon   sausage
cheese   salad   fork   egg   fish   knife

3. Read the comic again and answer the questions.

What does Jenny have on Wednesday?

She has a _____ and a _____ sandwich.

What does Jenny have on Friday?

She _____ and a _____ sandwich.

What does Jenny have every day?

She _____ every day.

Who likes ham sandwiches?

_____ likes ham sandwiches.

4. Colour the meals that Jenny doesn't eat and you'll find out what she likes best.

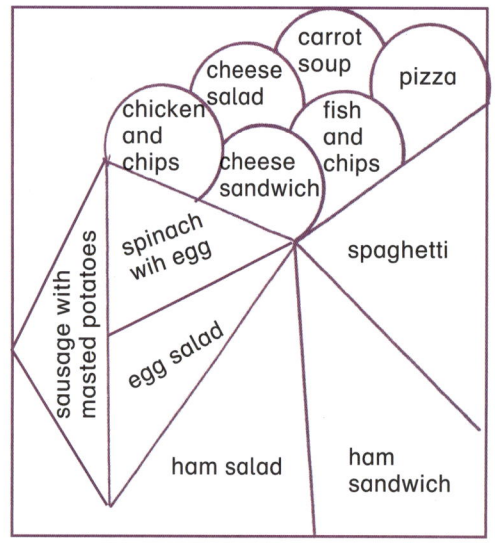

Male die Gerichte an, die Jenny nicht isst. Wenn du alles richtig machst, findest du heraus, was Jenny am liebsten mag.

Jenny likes _____ best. And you?

I like _____ best.

 Comic

Sally's daily routine

Another school day learning English, German and maths. From nine o'clock till twelve o'clock.

Lunch with Koala at one o'clock.

Sports in the afternoon at two o'clock, that's fun.

Homework at four o'clock, and then I can ride my bike.

At seven o'clock, I can watch a film on TV.

At eight o'clock it's time for bed.

Oh no, I'm late for school. I must run.

Another school day? Oh no, it isn't. It's Sunday today.

1. What does Tom do every day? Draw lines and write.

	five o'clock
	seven o'clock
	eight o'clock
	one o'clock
	three o'clock
	nine o'clock

I get up **at** seven o'clock.

_____

_____

_____

_____

_____

get up   go to bed and sleep   play with my friends
start school   have lunch   do my homework

16

2. Read the comic again and circle the correct answer.

Sally starts school at	eight o'clock. L nine o'clock. N
She has lunch at	one o'clock. I twelve o'clock. U
Sally can watch a film	in the morning. N in the evening. G
At eight o'clock, Sally	goes to bed. H has lunch. C
Today is	Sunday. T Monday. H

We sleep at _ _ _ _ _ .

3. Draw in the correct time. Number the pictures in the correct order.

📕 Comic

Sporty Sally

1. What are their favourite hobbies? Look and write.

Schaue in der Tabelle nach, welche Sportart sich hinter der Buchstaben-Ziffer-Kombination verbirgt und schreibe sie auf die Linie.

	1	2	3	4
A				
B				
C				

My favourite hobby is A2 _____.

My favourite hobby is C3 _____.

My favourite hobby is A4 _____.

My favourite hobby is B4 _____.

My favourite hobbies are B3 _____ and

C4 _____.

My favourite hobbies are A1 _____ and

C1 _____.

My favourite hobbies are B1 _____ and

C2 _____.

My favourite hobbies are A3 _____ and

B2 _____.

**playing basketball   playing tennis   riding a bike
playing football   riding a horse   inline skating
playing the guitar   ice skating   snowboarding
reading books   skateboarding   playing the piano**

19

✏ 2. Match the pictures with the correct speech bubble. Draw lines.

> We are going jumping.

> I'm going skateboarding.

> I'm going swimming.

> We love playing football and basketball.

✏ 3. Answer the question.

What's your favourite hobby?

 My favourite hobby is _____.

 My favourite hobby is _____.

 My favourite hobby is _____.

And my favourite hobby is _____.

 My favourite hobby is _____.

📕 Comic

Bad luck

🖊 1. Find the correct word. Fill in.

1 = w	7 = m	13 = i
2 = b	8 = p	14 = k
3 = s	9 = a	15 = c
4 = y	10 = h	16 = l
5 = u	11 = e	17 = o
6 = r	12 = t	

A) __ __ __ __ __ shop
   7 5 3 13 15

B) __ __ __ __ __ __ __ __ __ __ shop
   3 5 8 11 6 7 9 6 14 11 12

C) __ __ __ __ shop
   2 17 17 14

D) __ __ __ __ __ __ __ shop
   15 16 17 12 10 11 3

E) __ __ __ __ __ shop
   3 1 11 11 12

F) __ __ __ __ __ __ shop
   3 8 17 6 12 3

G) __ __ __ shop
   12 17 4

🖊 2. Fill in.

The hat is _____.

The hat is _____.

The hat is _____.

just right
too big
too small

3. What's missing? Look and write.

The _____
is missing.

The _____ are missing.

The _____ is missing.

4. What's wrong? Cross out.

Lilly and Joe **like / don't like** shopping.

They go to the **supermarket / music shop**.

Lilly buys a **magazine / CD**.

Joe buys inline skates in the

sports shop / clothes shop. In the

book shop / toy shop, they buy a book for

their **mother / father**. At home, they realize

that it was a **bad / good** shopping day.

📕 Comic

A trip through Sydney

1. What's wrong? Complete the sentences.

> Schau genau hin. Nicht alle Möbelstücke sind an ihrem richtigen Platz. Vervollständige die Sätze.

There's a __lamp__ in the __bathroom__ .

There's a __sofa__ in the __kitchen__ .

There's a __bed__ in the __living room__ .

There's a __cupboard__ in the __garden__ .

There's a __desk__ in the __toilet__ .

There's a __table__ in the __bedroom__ .

There's a __chair__ on the __stairs__ .

There are __shelves__ in the __garage__ .

| living room bedroom kitchen garden garage toilet stairs |
| bathroom lamp table bed sofa cupboard shelves desk chair |

2. Complete the sentences. Draw lines.

The shelves are — for the living room.

The cupboards are — too big.

The sofa is — for the kitchen.

The armchair is — for the bathroom.

1₂3. Complete the sentences and number.

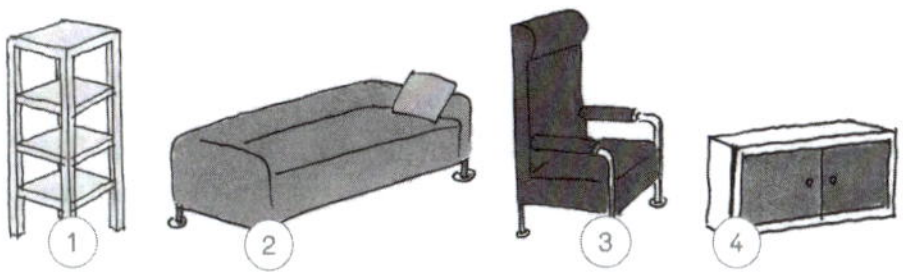

(3) I'd love to do my homework in this __armchair__ . It's so comfortable.

(2) Look at this fantastic __sofa__ .

(4) These __cupboards__ are great. I'll have enough room to play on the floor.

(1) Mum, look at these __shelves__ . They are really nice.

Comic

Jenny is hungry

Monday
EVERY DAY: ham sandwich or cheese sandwich
Today you can have carrot soup or chicken and chips.
carrot soup | chicken & chips
I'd like the carrot soup – and a ham sandwich, please.

Tuesday
EVERY DAY: ham sandwich or cheese sandwich
Today you can have cheese salad or spaghetti.
cheese salad | spaghetti
I'd like the spaghetti, please – and a ham sandwich.

Wednesday
EVERY DAY: ham sandwich or cheese sandwich
We have sausage with mashed potatoes today or pizza.
sausage with mashed potatoes | pizza
I'd like the pizza, please – and a ham sandwich.

Thursday
EVERY DAY: ham sandwich or cheese sandwich
Would you like ham salad or spinach with egg today?
ham salad | spinach with
I'd like the ham salad, please – and a ham sandwich.

Friday
EVERY DAY: ham sand... or
Fish and chips, please – and a ham sandwich.
Well, Jenny, don't you want a cheese sandwich for a change?
Stupid idea. Bobby doesn't like cheese.
Now what are you going to have today: fish and chips or egg salad?
chips | egg salad
No, thank you.

1. What do they like? Read, write and draw.

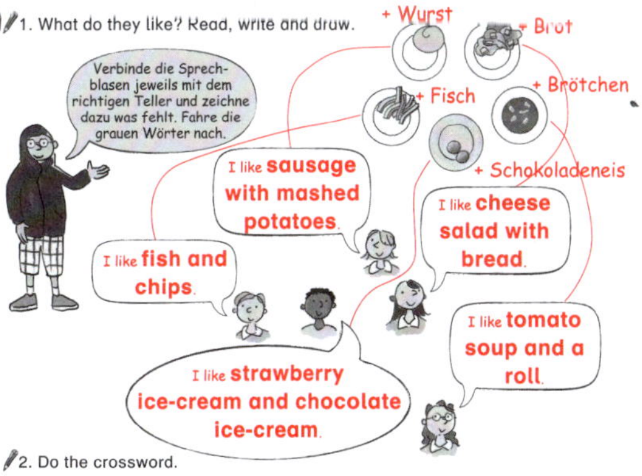

> Verbinde die Sprechblasen jeweils mit dem richtigen Teller und zeichne dazu was fehlt. Fahre die grauen Wörter nach.

+ Wurst
+ Brot
+ Fisch
+ Brötchen
+ Schokoladeneis

I like **sausage with mashed potatoes**

I like **cheese salad with bread**.

I like **fish and chips**.

I like **tomato soup and a roll**.

I like **strawberry ice-cream and chocolate ice-cream**.

2. Do the crossword.

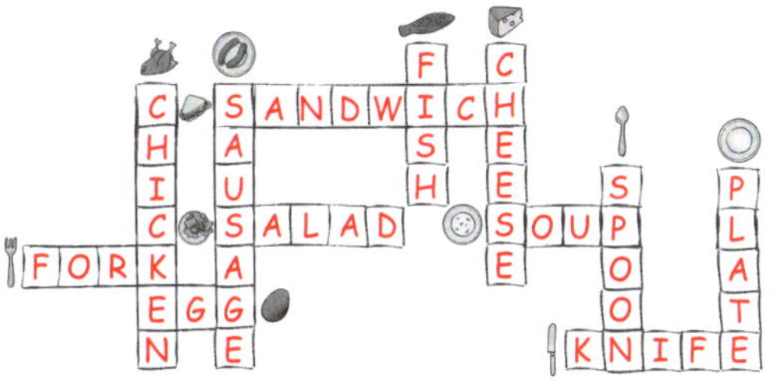

Crossword answers:
SANDWICH, CHEESE, CHICKEN, SAUSAGE, EGG, FORK, SALAD, FISH, SOUP, SPOON, PLATE, KNIFE

| sandwich plate soup chicken spoon sausage |
| cheese salad fork egg fish knife |

Lösungen

3. Read the comic again and answer the questions.

What does Jenny have on Wednesday?

She has a **pizza** and a **ham** sandwich.

What does Jenny have on Friday?

She **has fish and chips** and a **ham** sandwich.

What does Jenny have every day?

She **has a ham sandwich** every day.

Who likes ham sandwiches?

Bobby likes ham sandwiches.

4. Colour the meals that Jenny doesn't eat and you'll find out what she likes best.

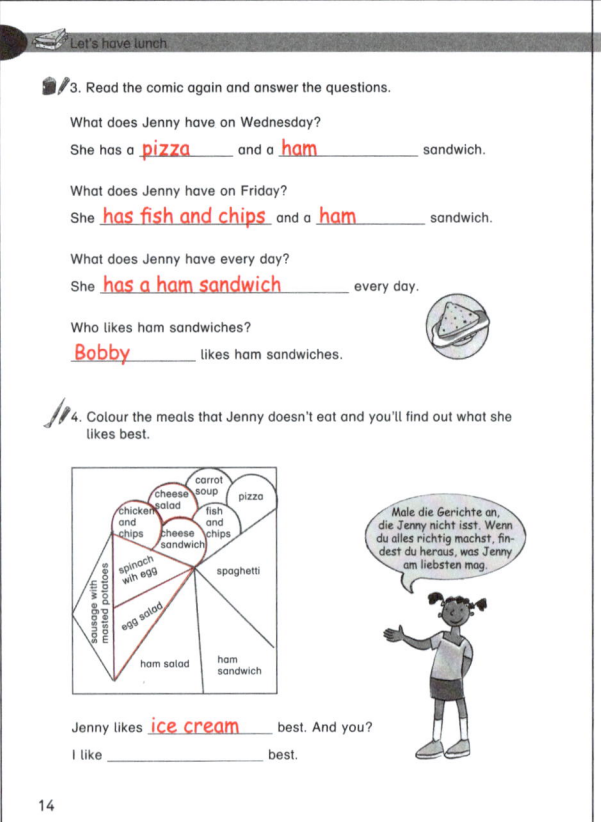

Male die Gerichte an, die Jenny nicht isst. Wenn du alles richtig machst, findest du heraus, was Jenny am liebsten mag.

Jenny likes **ice cream** best. And you?

I like _____ best.

Comic

Sally's daily routine

14

15

---

1. What does Tom do every day? Draw lines and write.

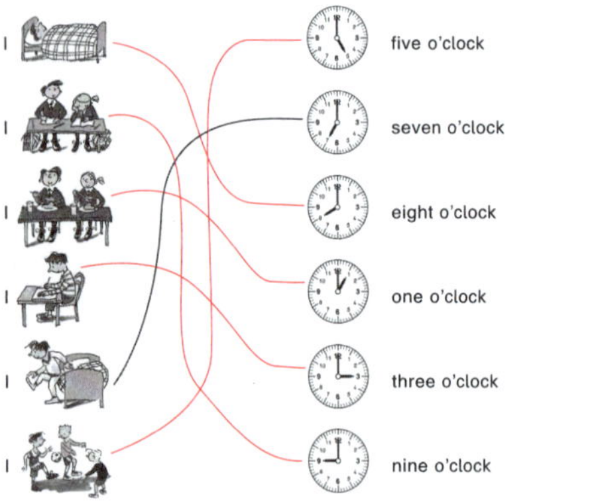

- five o'clock
- seven o'clock
- eight o'clock
- one o'clock
- three o'clock
- nine o'clock

I get up **at** seven o'clock.

I start school at nine o'clock.
I have lunch at one o'clock.
I do my homework at three o'clock.
I play with my friends at five o'clock.
I go to bed and sleep at eight o'clock.

get up   go to bed and sleep   play with my friends
start school   have lunch   do my homework

2. Read the comic again and circle the correct answer.

Sally starts school at	eight o'clock. L nine o'clock. (N)
She has lunch at	one o'clock. (I) twelve o'clock. U
Sally can watch a film	in the morning. N in the evening. (G)
At eight o'clock, Sally	goes to bed. (H) has lunch. C
Today is	Sunday. (T) Monday. H

We sleep at **NIGHT**.

3. Draw in the correct time. Number the pictures in the correct order.

②  ①

③

16

17

Comic

Sporty Sally

1. What are their favourite hobbies? Look and write.

Schaue in der Tabelle nach, welche Sportart sich hinter der Buchstaben-Ziffer-Kombination verbirgt und schreibe sie auf die Linie.

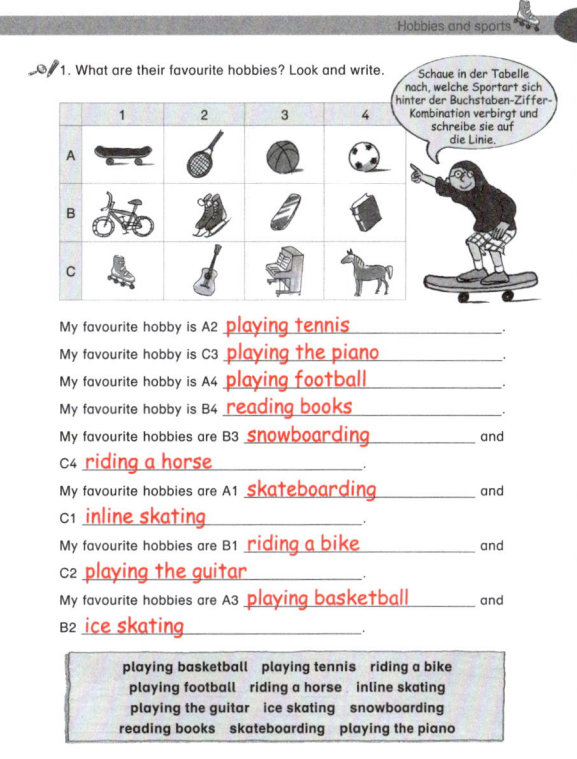

	1	2	3	4
A				
B				
C				

My favourite hobby is A2 **playing tennis** .
My favourite hobby is C3 **playing the piano** .
My favourite hobby is A4 **playing football** .
My favourite hobby is B4 **reading books** .
My favourite hobbies are B3 **snowboarding** and
C4 **riding a horse** .
My favourite hobbies are A1 **skateboarding** and
C1 **inline skating** .
My favourite hobbies are B1 **riding a bike** and
C2 **playing the guitar** .
My favourite hobbies are A3 **playing basketball** and
B2 **ice skating** .

playing basketball   playing tennis   riding a bike
playing football   riding a horse   inline skating
playing the guitar   ice skating   snowboarding
reading books   skateboarding   playing the piano

2. Match the pictures with the correct speech bubble. Draw lines.

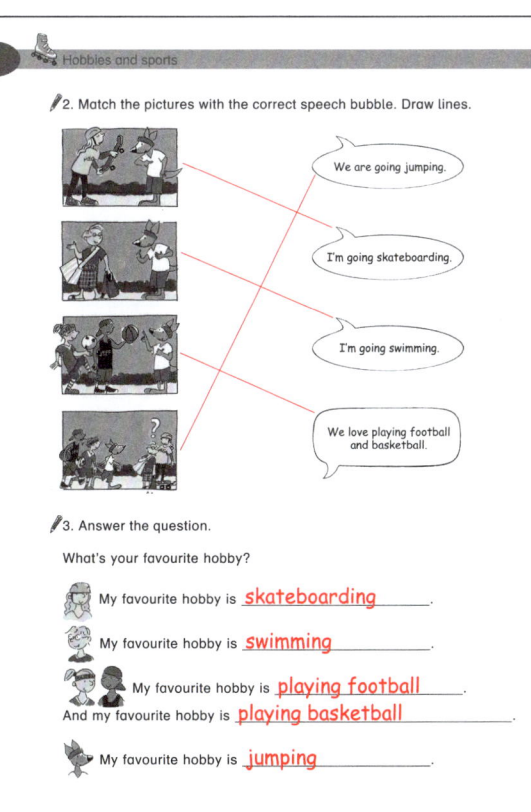

We are going jumping.

I'm going skateboarding.

I'm going swimming.

We love playing football and basketball.

3. Answer the question.

What's your favourite hobby?

My favourite hobby is **skateboarding** .

My favourite hobby is **swimming** .

My favourite hobby is **playing football** .
And my favourite hobby is **playing basketball**

My favourite hobby is **jumping** .

Comic

Bad luck

Lösungen

1. Find the correct word. Fill in.

1 = w	7 = m	13 = i
2 = b	8 = p	14 = k
3 = s	9 = a	15 = c
4 = y	10 = h	16 = l
5 = u	11 = e	17 = o
6 = r	12 = t	

A **music** shop
7 5 3 13 15

B **supermarket**
3 5 8 11 6 7 9 6 14 11 12

C **book** shop
2 17 17 14

D **clothes** shop
15 16 17 12 10 11 3

E **sweet** shop
3 1 11 11 12

F **sports** shop
3 8 17 6 12 3

G **toy** shop
12 17 4

2. Fill in.

The hat is **too small**.

The hat is **too big**.

The hat is **just right**.

> just right
> too big
> too small

3. What's missing? Look and write.

The **book shop** is missing.

The **inline skates** are missing.

The **CD** is missing.

4. What's wrong? Cross out.

Lilly and Joe like/~~don't like~~ shopping.

They go to the ~~supermarket~~/music shop.

Lilly buys a ~~magazine~~/CD.

Joe buys inline skates in the

sports shop/~~clothes shop~~. In the

book shop/~~toy shop~~ they buy a book for

their mother/~~father~~. At home they realize

that it was a bad/~~good~~ shopping day.

22

23

Comic

A trip through Sydney

24

1. Do the crossword.

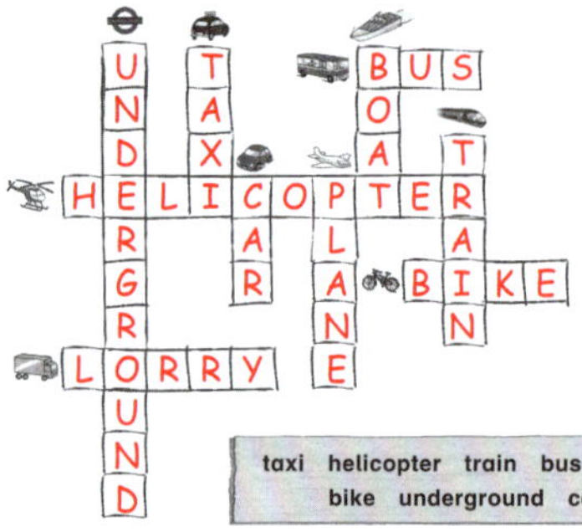

> taxi helicopter train bus lorry plane
> bike underground car boat

2. Where are they going to? Draw and complete the sentences.

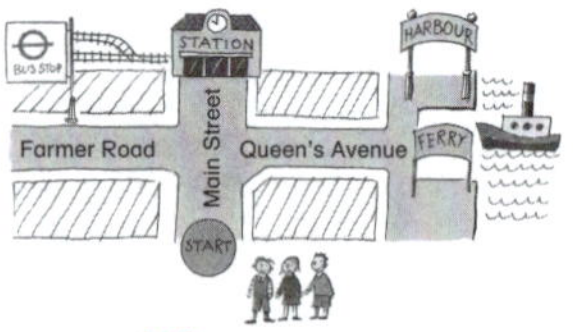

> Schau dir die Sätze
> und die Karte genau an. Fahre
> den Weg jedes Kindes nach.
> Ergänze dann die Sätze.

John turns **left** into Farmer Road and goes to the

bus stop.

Mary turns **right** into Queen's Avenue and goes to the

ferry wharf.

Ben goes **straight on** to the **train** station.

25

Page 26

✏ 3. Draw and write.

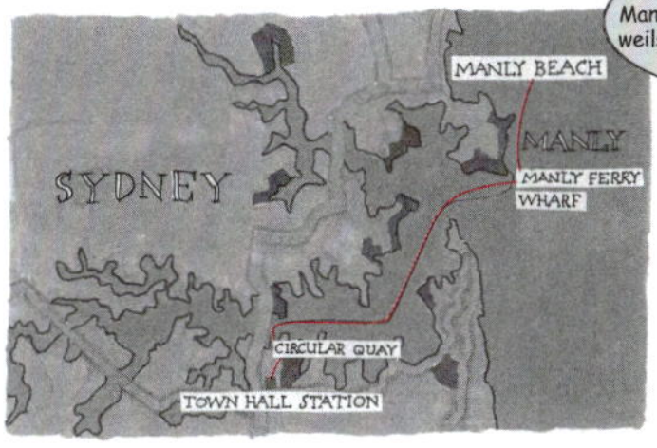

Zeichne Sallys Weg nach Manly Beach ein. Schreibe jeweils dazu, welches Verkehrsmittel Sally nimmt.

1. train   2. ferry   3. bus

1₂3̶4. Number the sentences in the correct order.

⑤ Just turn around!

② Walk straight on to the ferry wharf.

⑥ What a trip! I'm glad I found you. But I love the beach!

① Take the train to Circular Quay.

④ Excuse me, how do I get to the beach?

③ Turn right into South Esplanade.

Page 27

📖 Comic

Monkey party

Page 28

👁✏ 1. Find the words and draw lines.

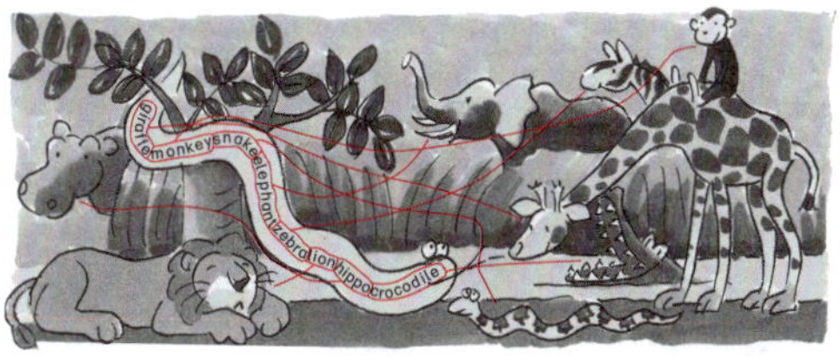

👁✏ 2. What animal is it? Look and write.

crocodile   hippo   snake

elephant   monkey   lion

Hey, that's my arm.   Aaargh, my foot.

koala lion kangaroo hippo elephant
crocodile snake monkey

And who is this? Koala and Sally, the kangaroo.

Page 29

✏ 3. Correct or wrong? Tick.

Wenn du alles richtig gemacht hast, ergeben die Buchstaben das Lösungswort in der Sprechblase.

Happy birthday!

	correct	wrong
The zebra is very fast.	h	c
The lion is very strong.	a	r
The snake is very funny.	u	p
The monkeys are very long.	k	p
The giraffe is very tall.	y	e

1₂3✏ 4. Number in the correct order and write.

② Zorro, the zebra

③ Giro, the giraffe

⑤ Lollo, the lion

④ Sila, the snake

① Milli, the monkey

In welcher Reihenfolge kommen die Gäste zur Geburtstagsfeier?

Lösungen

Comic

What's wrong with Sally?

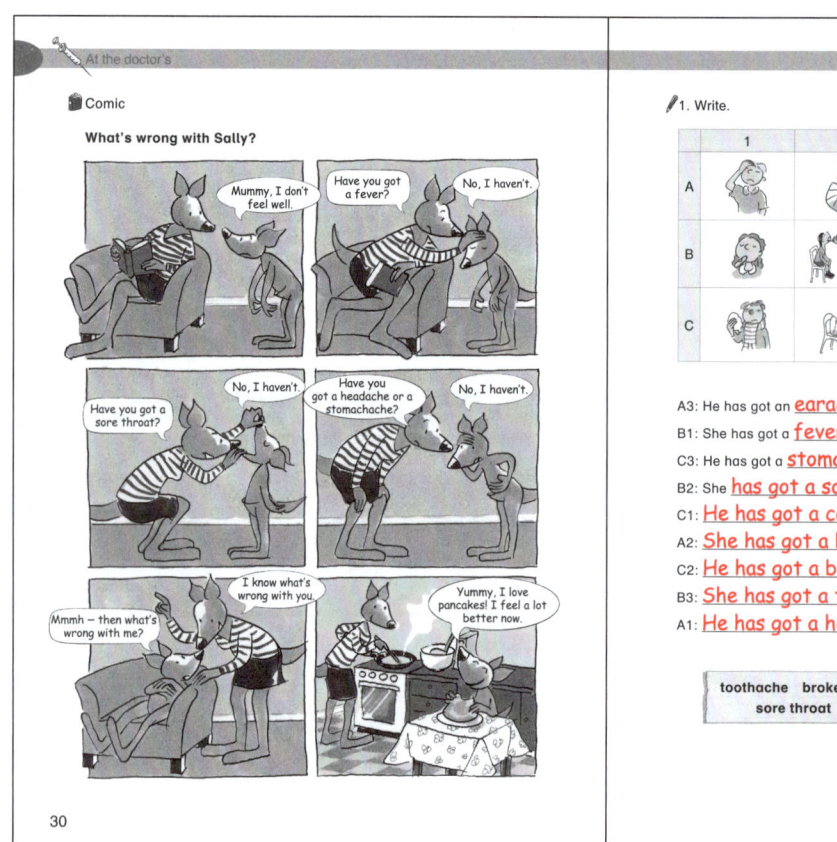

✏ 1. Write.

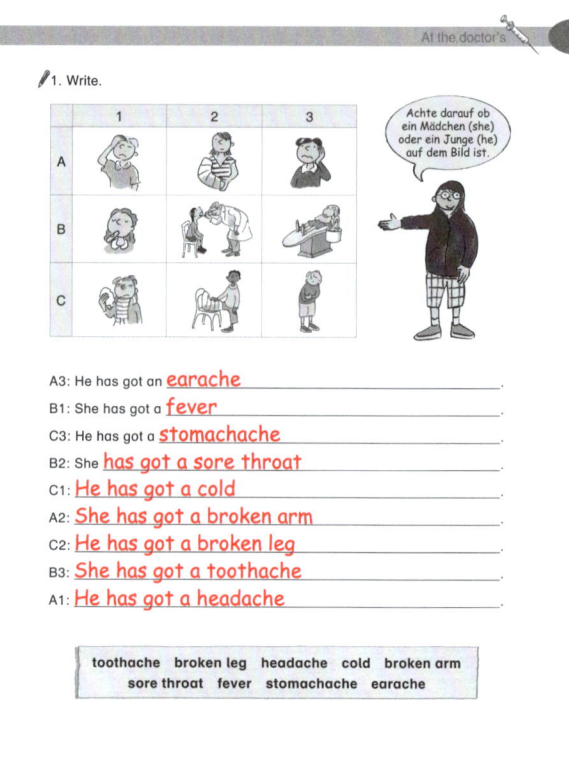

Achte darauf ob ein Mädchen (she) oder ein Junge (he) auf dem Bild ist.

A3: He has got an **earache** .
B1: She has got a **fever** .
C3: He has got a **stomachache** .
B2: She **has got a sore throat** .
C1: **He has got a cold** .
A2: **She has got a broken arm** .
C2: **He has got a broken leg** .
B3: **She has got a toothache** .
A1: **He has got a headache** .

toothache   broken leg   headache   cold   broken arm
sore throat   fever   stomachache   earache

1₂3 ✏ 2. Number the pictures in the correct order and draw lines.

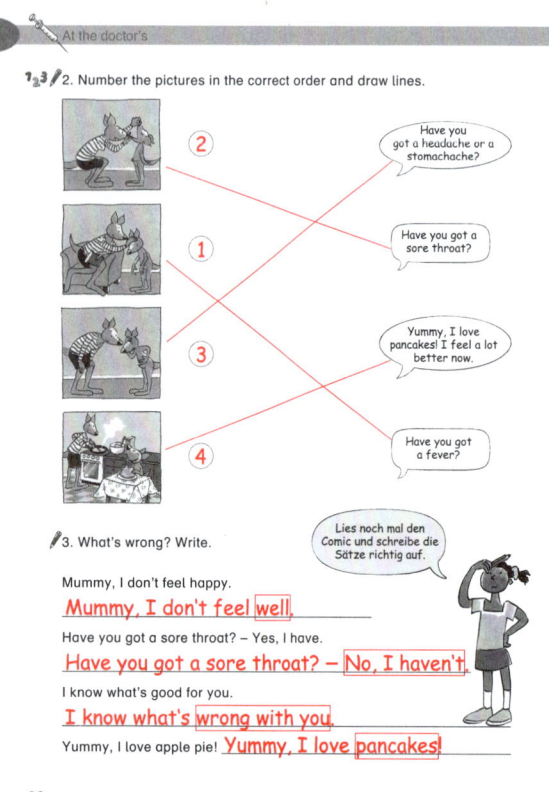

✏ 3. What's wrong? Write.

Lies noch mal den Comic und schreibe die Sätze richtig auf.

Mummy, I don't feel happy.
Mummy, I don't feel well.

Have you got a sore throat? – Yes, I have.
Have you got a sore throat? – No, I haven't.

I know what's good for you.
I know what's wrong with you.

Yummy, I love apple pie! **Yummy, I love pancakes!**

Comic

Tim is busy

Jobs

1. Trace the lines and write.

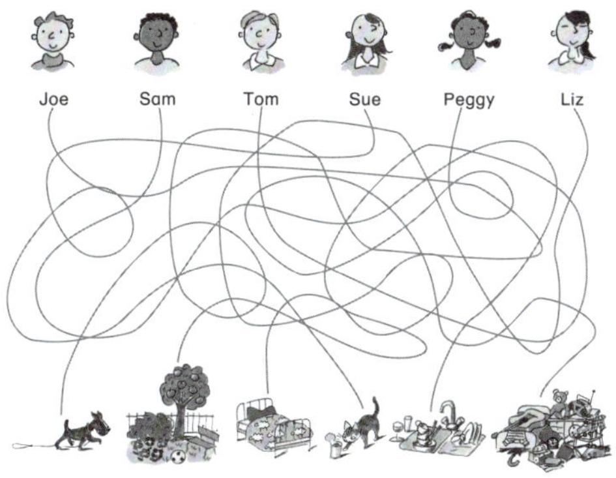

Joe   Sam   Tom   Sue   Peggy   Liz

walk the dog   make the bed   help in the kitchen
help in the garden   tidy her room   feed the cat

Joe has to **walk the dog**.
Sam has to **help in the kitchen**.
Tom has to help in the garden.
Sue has to feed the cat.
Peggy has to tidy her room.
Liz has to make the bed.

34

2. Answer the questions. Cross out.

Streiche jeweils die falsche Antwort durch.

Is Tim lazy?   Yes, he is. / ~~No, he isn't.~~

Does he help his mother in the garden?   ~~Yes, he does.~~ / No, he doesn't.

Is Tim's mother angry?   Yes, she is. / ~~No, she isn't.~~

Does Tim want to go to Auntie Jane?   ~~Yes, he does.~~ / No, he doesn't.

3. Correct the sentences.

Make the dog. **Walk the dog.**
Help me in the cat. **Help me in the kitchen.**
Feed the kitchen. **Feed the cat.**
Walk your bed. **Make your bed.**

35

Meeting people

Comic

Sally at the International Summer Camp

36

1. Write and draw lines.

Trage erst die Länder ein und verbinde dann mit der richtigen Flagge.

Great Britain   Greece
Germany   Spain
Australia   France
Poland   Italy
Turkey
USA   Russia

Great Britain Australia USA Poland Germany
Turkey Russia Spain France Italy Greece

37

Lösungen

2. Correct or wrong? Circle the correct letter.

	correct	wrong
Sally gives out buttons with the American flag on them.	P	(G)
Süheyl is from Turkey.	(R)	O
Sally and Koala visit the camp together.	(E)	L
Juanita is from Italy.	A	(E)
Stefan welcomes Sally and Koala.	(C)	N
They meet at the "International Winter Camp".	D	(E)

Draw the flag. It's the flag of __Greece__ .

3. Where do the children come from? Draw lines.

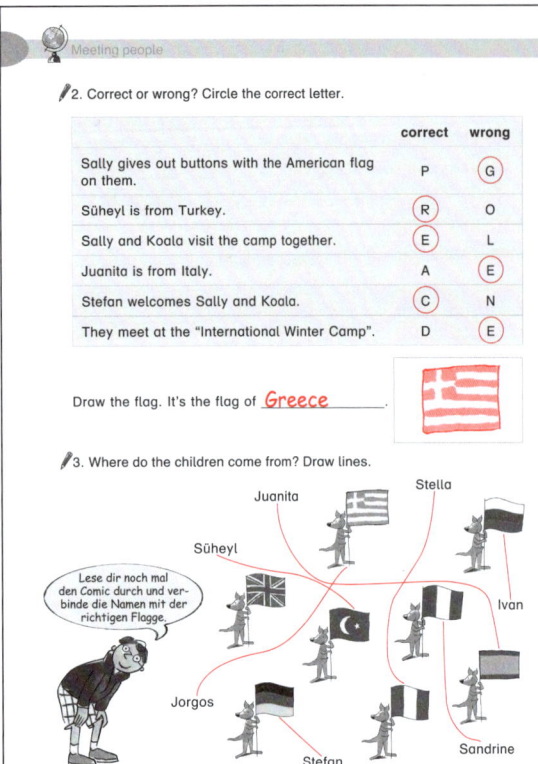

Lese dir noch mal den Comic durch und verbinde die Namen mit der richtigen Flagge.

Juanita Stella Süheyl Ivan Jorgos Stefan Sandrine

38

Comic

Holiday planning

39

---

1. Write down the names of the sights.

Statue of Liberty

Grand Canyon

Golden Gate Bridge

Mississippi River

> Golden Gate Bridge   Mississippi River
> Statue of Liberty   Grand Canyon

2. Some information about the USA. Cross out.

Streiche jeweils die falsche Ergänzung durch.

The USA are a very ~~small~~ / big country. The flag is called "Stars and Stripes" and it's blue, red and white / ~~black, red and white~~. In the USA you pay with dollars / ~~euros~~. The longest river is the ~~Missouri River~~ / Mississippi River. The Golden Gate Bridge is in San Francisco / ~~New York~~. The Statue of Liberty holds a ~~big ice cream~~ / a torch and a book in her hands.

40

3. Look at the comic. Draw lines and write.

I'd like to see __the Golden Gate Bridge__ .

I'd like to see __the Grand Canyon__ .

I'd like to see __the Mississippi River__ .

I'd like to see __the Statue of Liberty__ .

I'd like to buy __a swimming pool__ .

41

Halloween

Comic

Sally's Halloween

Hey, it's Halloween! I love going from door to door in a costume. It's funny to scare other people.

And I love saying "Trick or Treat" and getting lots of sweets.

Hmmm ... I don't know. Let's go and try some costumes.

What would you like to be at Halloween?

But you don't look scary at all. I want to be a Jack O'Lantern.

Nobody will be scared of you in a vampire costume.

Boo! I'm a wicked witch.

But what's that, Sally, where's your costume? Nobody will be scared of a kangaroo.

AAAH!

But they will be scared of a kangaroo's skeleton, ha ha ha.

Maybe a bat? — No, that's too black. Maybe a ghost? — No, that's too white... I have an idea!

Turn off the light, Koala!

42

Halloween

1. Find the words and circle them.

a	d	w	o	g	h	o	s	t	k	x	f	s
j	h	n	k	a	n	b	j	v	w	v	b	k
t	r	i	c	k	o	r	t	r	e	a	t	e
l	c	g	c	s	t	o	y	s	p	m	i	l
z	e	h	o	b	a	b	a	t	d	p	m	e
w	i	t	c	h	i	v	a	d	f	i	k	t
q	v	o	w	l	m	h	r	e	b	r	n	o
t	j	a	c	k	o	l	a	n	t	e	r	n

Suche die Wörter senkrecht und waagrecht. Kreise sie ein.

night   witch   ghost   Trick or Treat
vampire   skeleton   bat   Jack O'Lantern

2. Fill in the missing words.

It's Halloween. It's a dark **night**.

The candles are shining in the **Jack O'Lantern**.

A **witch** is crossing the street.

A **bat** is flying around.

A **vampire** is hiding behind a bush.

A **skeleton** is clattering with its bones.

A **ghost** is shouting "Boo!"

The creatures meet in front of a house and ring the bell.

The door opens and they shout out loud: " **Trick or Treat** !"

43

Halloween

3. Number the speech bubbles in the correct order.

Turn off the light, Koala! 5

I have an idea! 3

Nobody will be scared of you in a vampire costume. 2

I don't know. Let's go and try some costumes. 1

But what's that, Sally, where's your costume? 4

Streiche die falsche Ergänzung durch.

4. Cross out.

Koala wants to be ~~a vampire~~ / a Jack O'Lantern.

Sally ~~likes~~ / doesn't like the bat costume.

Koala has to turn off the light to see Sally's skeleton costume / ~~ghost costume~~.

Sally and Koala are trying some costumes ~~at home~~ / in a shop.

What would you like to be at Halloween?

I would like to be a _____.

44

Christmas

Comic

A surprise for Father Christmas

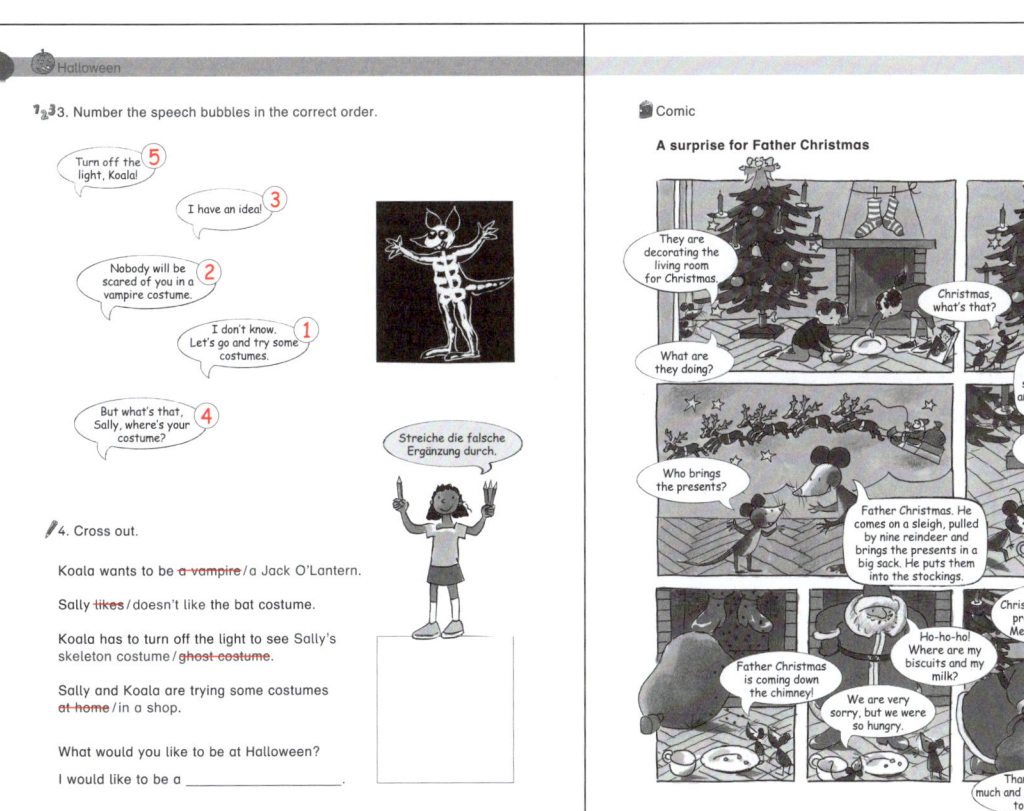

They are decorating the living room for Christmas.

What are they doing?

Christmas, what's that?

Look, people have a Christmas tree with stars, candles and bells and an angel on top. They get presents, too.

Who brings the presents?

Look, Mummy, milk and biscuits. I'm so hungry.

Father Christmas. He comes on a sleigh, pulled by nine reindeer and brings the presents in a big sack. He puts them into the stockings.

Well, it's Christmas. This is my present for you. Merry Christmas!

Father Christmas is coming down the chimney!

Ho-ho-ho! Where are my biscuits and my milk?

We are very sorry, but we were so hungry.

Thank you very much and merry Christmas to you, too.

45

Lösungen

✏️ 1. What can you see on the Christmas branch? Look, write and draw.

Schreibe die Wörter anhand der Tabelle. Male die letzten beiden Bilder selbst.

1 = a	5 = e	9 = i	13 = n	17 = s
2 = b	6 = f	10 = k	14 = o	18 = t
3 = c	7 = g	11 = l	15 = p	
4 = d	8 = h	12 = m	16 = r	

① **candle**
 3 1 13 4 11 5

② **Father Christmas**
 6 1 18 8 5 16   3 8 16 9 17 18 12 1 17

③ **present**
 15 16 5 17 5 13 18

④ **stocking**
 17 18 14 3 10 9 13 7

⑤ **angel**
 1 13 7 5 11

⑥ **bell**
 2 5 11 11

⑦ **star**
 17 18 1 16

46

✏️ 2. Correct or wrong? Circle the correct letter and find the word.

	correct	wrong
The milk and biscuits are for Father Christmas.	(B)	S
There are toys on the Christmas tree.	T	(E)
Father Christmas comes in a helicopter.	A	(L)
The presents are in a sack.	(L)	R

The word is: **b e l l**

📖 3. Read the comic again and fill in the missing words.

People have a Christmas tree with **s t a r s , c a n d l e s** and **b e l l s** and an **a n g e l** on top.

Who brings the **p r e s e n t s** ? Father Christmas.

He comes on a **s l e i g h** pulled by nine **r e i n d e e r** .

Father Christmas comes down the **c h i m n e y** .

He says:

> **Merry Christmas to you** !

47

Look at the comics again. Find the missing words and write them into the squares. The letters in the marked squares form a sentence.

Trage die fehlenden Wörter in die Kästchen ein. Die Buchstaben in den markierten Feldern ergeben einen Satz.

Comic 1: We had a great **t i m e** at the beach.
 1

Comic 2: Who's **c o u n t i n g** there?
 2

Comic 3: The **s o f a** is for the living room.
 3

Comic 4: I'd like the carrot soup – and a ham **s a n d w i c h** , please.
 4

Comic 5: It's **S u n d a y** today.
 5

Comic 6: No thanks, I prefer **j u m p i n g** .
 6

Comic 7: Oh no, the **i n l i n e** skates are too big.
 7

Comic 8: Walk **s t r a i g h t** on to the ferry wharf.
 8

Comic 9: This is Sila, the **s n a k e** .
 9

Comic 10: Have you got a **h e a d a c h e** or a stomachache?
 10

Comic 11: Help me in the **k i t c h e n** , please.
 11

Comic 12: I'm Jorgos from **G r e e c e** .
 12

Comic 13: I'd like to see the Statue of **L i b e r t y** .
 13

Comic 14: I'm a wicked **w i t c h** .
 14

Comic 15: Father **C h r i s t m a s** is coming
 15
down the **c h i m n e y** .
 16

> **I can**
> 1 2 3 4
> **speak**
> 5 6 7 8 9
> **English.**
> 10 11 12 13 14 15 16

48

✏ 1. Do the crossword.

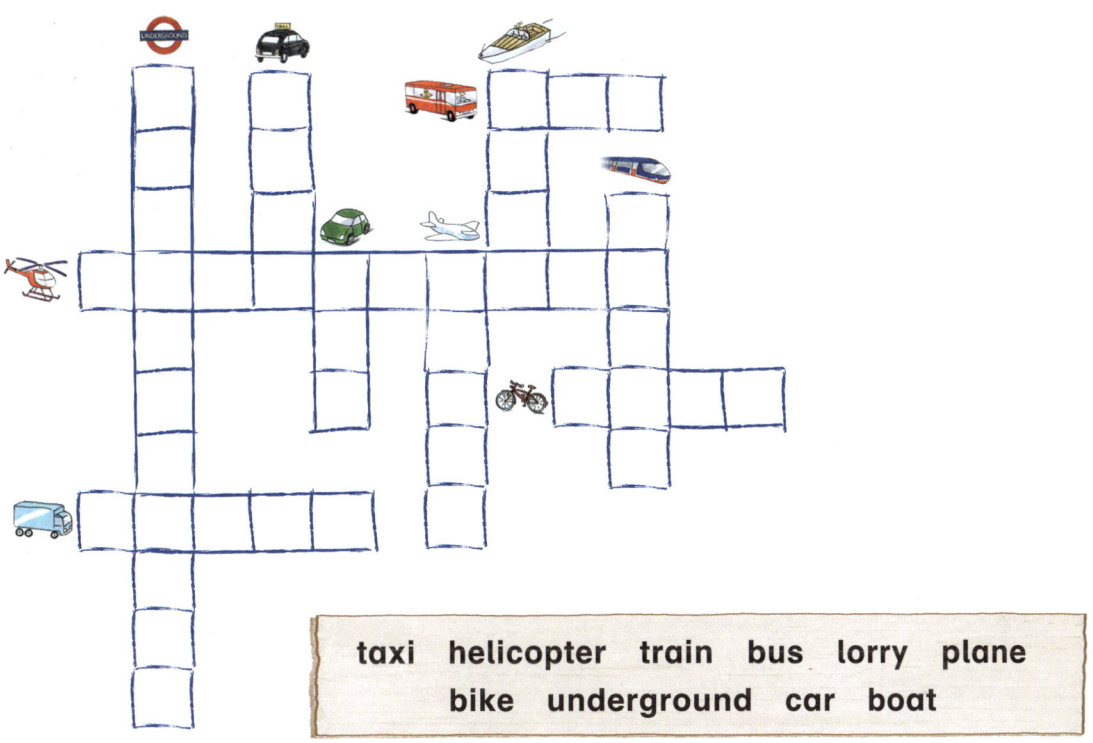

| taxi   helicopter   train   bus   lorry   plane |
| bike   underground   car   boat |

✏ 2. Where are they going to? Draw and complete the sentences.

Schau dir die Sätze und die Karte genau an. Fahre den Weg jedes Kindes nach. Ergänze dann die Sätze.

John turns _____ into Farmer Road and goes to the

_____ stop.

Mary turns _____ into Queen's Avenue and goes to the

_____ wharf.

Ben goes _____ to the _____ station.

3. Draw and write.

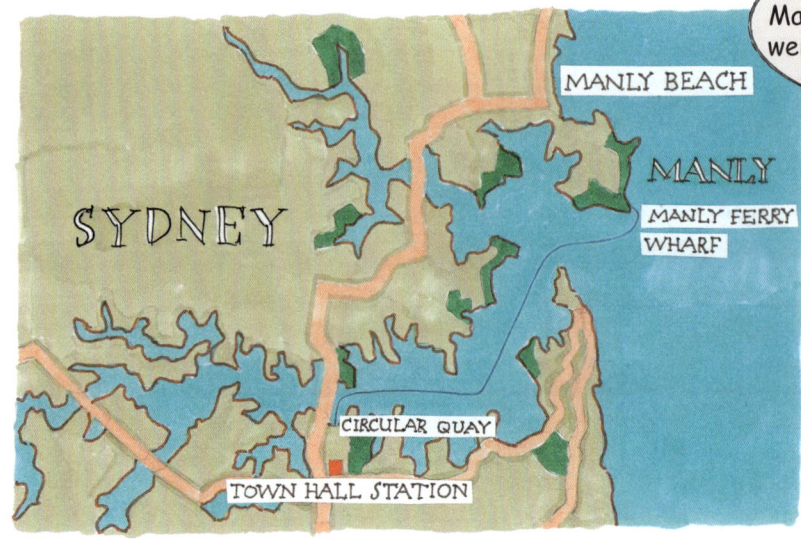

Zeichne Sallys Weg nach Manly Beach ein. Schreibe jeweils dazu, welches Verkehrsmittel Sally nimmt.

1. _____   2. _____   3. _____

4. Number the sentences in the correct order.

◯ Just turn around!

◯ Walk straight on to the ferry wharf.

◯ What a trip! I'm glad I found you. But I love the beach!

◯ Take the train to Circular Quay.

◯ Excuse me, how do I get to the beach?

◯ Turn right into South Esplanade.

📕 Comic

Monkey party

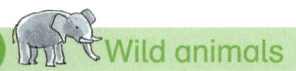
1. Find the words and draw lines.

2. What animal is it? Look and write.

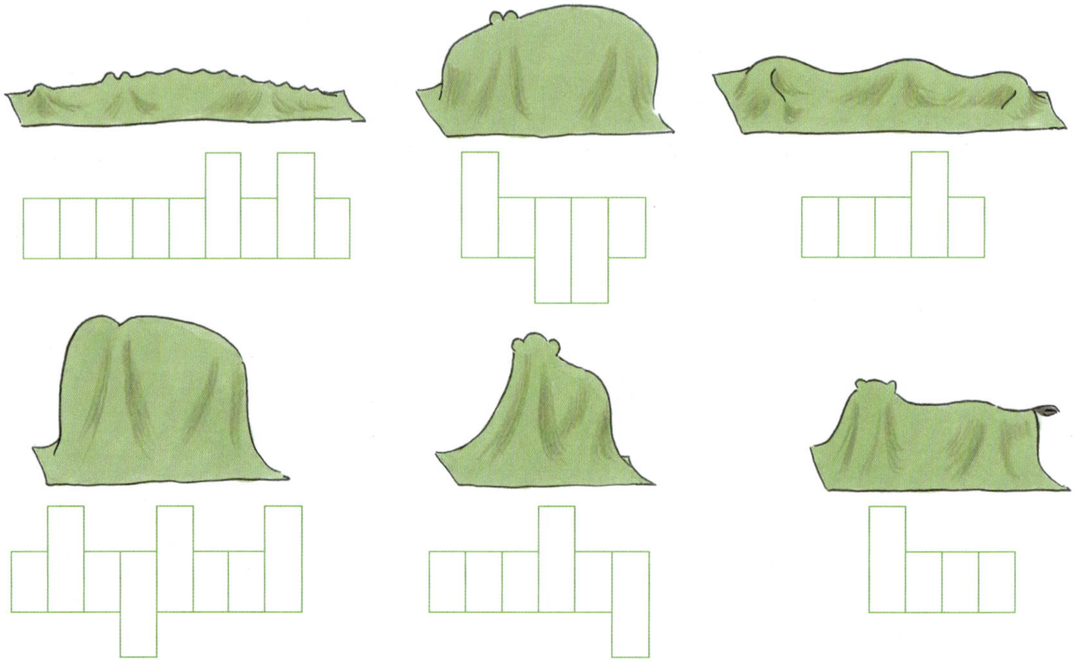

koala   lion   kangaroo   hippo   elephant
crocodile   snake   monkey

Hey, that's my arm.

Aaargh, my foot.

And who is this? _____ and _____, the _____.

3. Correct or wrong? Tick.

Wenn du alles richtig gemacht hast, ergeben die Buchstaben das Lösungswort in der Sprechblase.

	correct	wrong
The zebra is very fast.	h	c
The lion is very strong.	a	r
The snake is very funny.	u	p
The monkeys are very long.	k	p
The giraffe is very tall.	y	e

_____ birthday!

4. Number in the correct order and write.

 Zorro, the _____

 Giro, the _____

 Lollo, the _____

 Sila, the _____

 Milli, the _____

In welcher Reihenfolge kommen die Gäste zur Geburtstagsfeier?

📕 Comic

What's wrong with Sally?

1. Write.

	1	2	3
A			
B			
C			

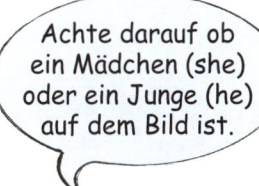

Achte darauf ob ein Mädchen (she) oder ein Junge (he) auf dem Bild ist.

A3: He has got an _____.

B1: She has got a _____.

C3: He has got a _____.

B2: She _____.

C1: _____.

A2: _____.

C2: _____.

B3: _____.

A1: _____.

toothache   broken leg   headache   cold   broken arm
sore throat   fever   stomachache   earache

31

123 🖊 2. Number the pictures in the correct order and draw lines.

Have you got a headache or a stomachache?

Have you got a sore throat?

Yummy, I love pancakes! I feel a lot better now.

Have you got a fever?

Lies noch mal den Comic und schreibe die Sätze richtig auf.

🖊 3. What's wrong? Write.

Mummy, I don't feel happy.

_____

Have you got a sore throat? – Yes, I have.

_____

I know what's good for you.

_____

Yummy, I love apple pie! _____

📕 Comic

Tim is busy

Tim, look at your room. You really have to tidy it. And you have to make your bed.

Tim, you are so lazy. Help me in the kitchen, please.

Tim, you are so lazy. Help me in the garden, please. Feed the cat, please. And walk the dog, please.

And what about your homework?

Tim, come on. We have to go to Auntie Jane's tea party.

Sorry Mum, I'm too busy: I have to tidy my room, clean the kitchen, work in the garden,...

1. Trace the lines and write.

| Joe | Sam | Tom | Sue | Peggy | Liz |

| walk the dog | make the bed | help in the kitchen |
| help in the garden | tidy her room | feed the cat |

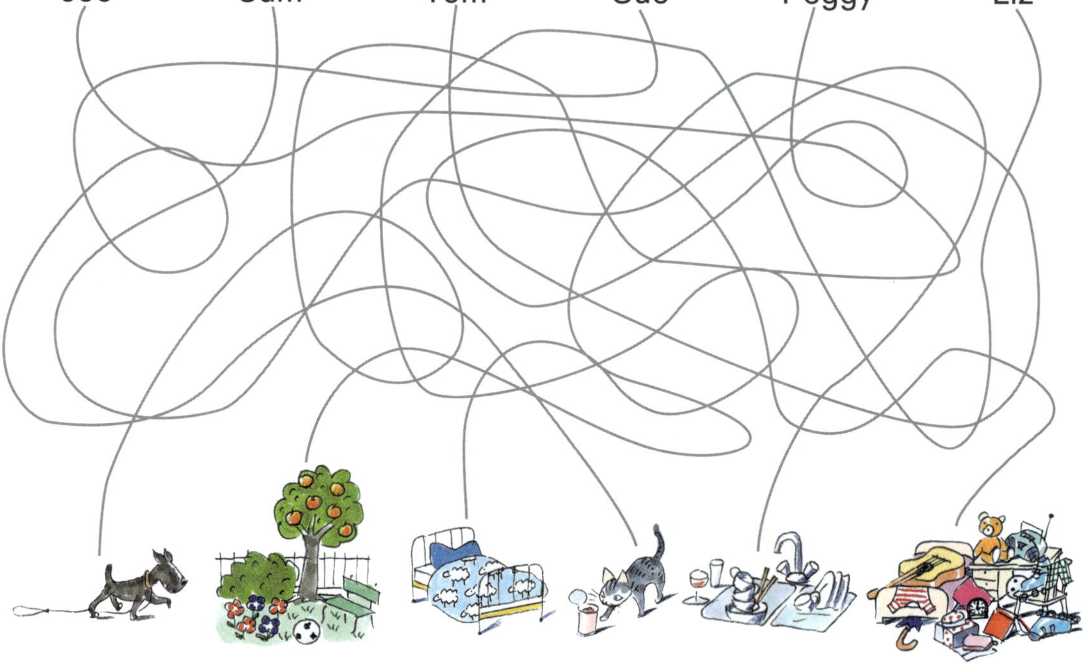

Joe has to _____.

Sam has to _____.

_____.

_____.

_____.

_____.

🖊 2. Answer the questions. Cross out.

Streiche jeweils die falsche Antwort durch.

Is Tim lazy?	Yes, he is. / No, he isn't.
Does he help his mother in the garden?	Yes, he does. / No, he doesn't.
Is Tim's mother angry?	Yes, she is. / No, she isn't.
Does Tim want to go to Auntie Jane?	Yes, he does. / No, he doesn't.

🖊 3. Correct the sentences.

Walk

~~Make~~ the dog. ___Walk the dog._____

Help me in the cat. _____

Feed the kitchen. _____

Walk your bed. _____

35

📕 Comic

Sally at the International Summer Camp

Koala, finally, holidays. Tomorrow we are going to the "International Summer Camp".

And we need lots of buttons with the Australian flag on them.

I'm so excited. We will make lots of new friends.

Hello, I'm Stefan from Germany. Welcome to the camp! Are you from Australia?

Hello, yes, we are. Here's a button for you.

I'm Juanita from Spain. Can we help you?

Thank you so much. And here are some buttons for you.

I'm Jorgos from Greece.

I'm Sandrine from France.

I'm Ivan from Russia.

Yes, of course. We are from Australia — here are some buttons for you.

I'm Stella from Italy.

I'm Süheyl from Turkey. May we sit here?

It's so great here. And look at the people, Koala, now they are all from Australia, too.

1. Write and draw lines.

> Trage erst die Länder ein und verbinde dann mit der richtigen Flagge.

**Great Britain   Australia   USA   Poland   Germany
Turkey   Russia   Spain   France   Italy   Greece**

2. Correct or wrong? Circle the correct letter.

	correct	wrong
Sally gives out buttons with the American flag on them.	P	G
Süheyl is from Turkey.	R	O
Sally and Koala visit the camp together.	E	L
Juanita is from Italy.	A	E
Stefan welcomes Sally and Koala.	C	N
They meet at the "International Winter Camp".	D	E

Draw the flag. It's the flag of _____.

3. Where do the children come from? Draw lines.

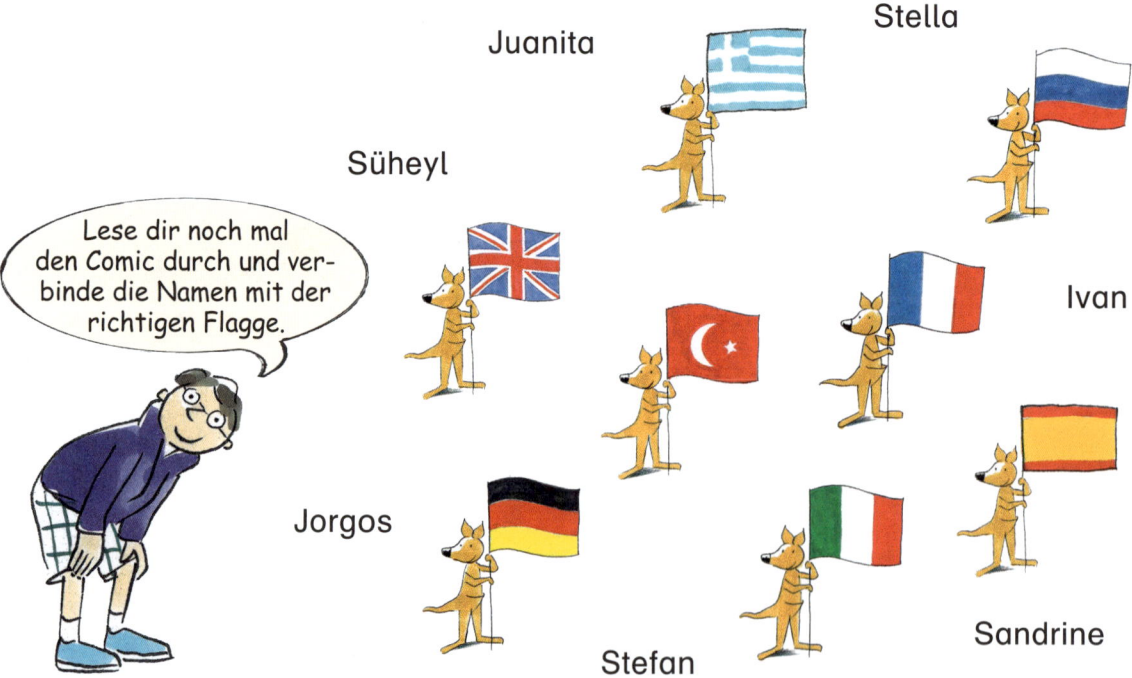

📕 Comic

Holiday planning

Let's plan our summer holidays. Where do you want to go?

I'd like to see the Grand Canyon.

I'd like to see the Golden Gate Bridge in San Francisco.

I'd like to go on a boat trip on the Mississippi River.

I'd like to see the Statue of Liberty in New York.

What would you like to do then?

I'd like to buy a swimming pool and stay at home with you.

Oh, the United States are too big. We can't visit all of these sights by car in one week.

Yippee! Such a great idea!

✏️ 1. Write down the names of the sights.

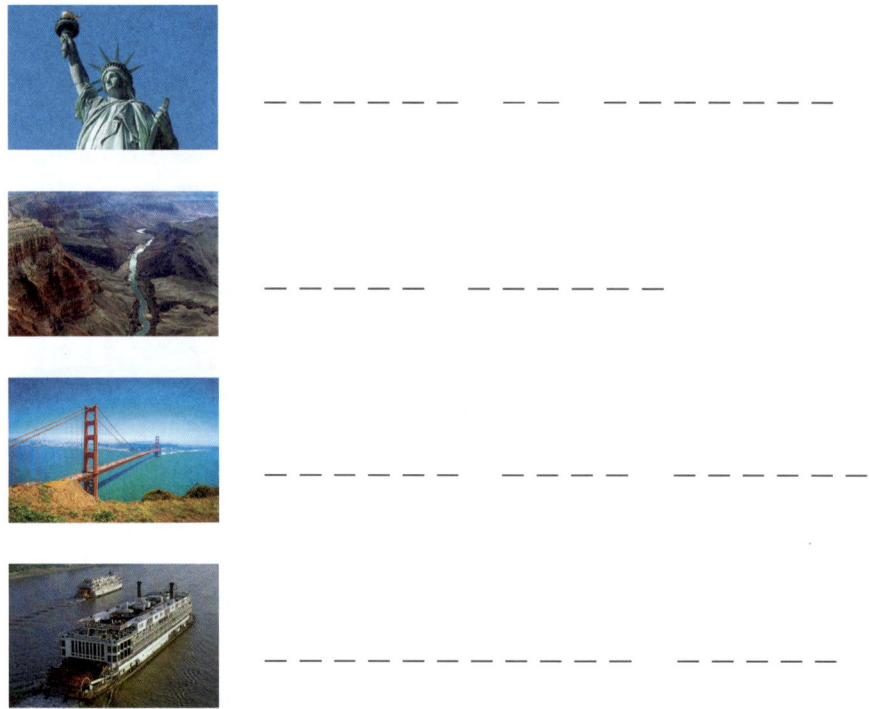

_ _ _ _ _ _ _ _ _ _ _ _ _

_ _ _ _ _ _ _ _ _

_ _ _ _ _ _ _ _ _ _ _ _ _ _

_ _ _ _ _ _ _ _ _ _ _ _ _ _

| Golden Gate Bridge | Mississippi River |
| Statue of Liberty | Grand Canyon |

✏️ 2. Some information about the USA. Cross out.

The USA are a very small / big country.
The flag is called "Stars and Stripes"
and it's blue, red and white / black,
red and white. In the USA you
pay with dollars / euros. The
longest river is the Missouri
River / Mississippi River.
The Golden Gate Bridge
is in San Francisco / New
York. The Statue of Liberty
holds a big ice cream / a
torch and a book in her hands.

Streiche jeweils
die falsche Ergänzung
durch.

3. Look at the comic. Draw lines and write.

 I'd like to see

_____.

 I'd like to see

_____.

 I'd like to see

_____.

 I'd like to see

_____.

 I'd like to buy

_____.

📕 Comic

Sally's Halloween

Hey, it's Halloween! I love going from door to door in a costume. It's funny to scare other people.

And I love saying "Trick or Treat" and getting lots of sweets.

Hmmm ... I don't know. Let's go and try some costumes.

What would you like to be at Halloween?

Boo! I'm a wicked witch.

But you don't look scary at all. I like this costume; I want to be a Jack O'Lantern.

Nobody will be scared of you in a vampire costume.

But what's that, Sally, where's your costume? Nobody will be scared of a kangaroo.

But they will be scared of a kangaroo's skeleton, ha ha ha.

Maybe a bat? — No, that's too black. Maybe a ghost? — No, that's too white... I have an idea!

Turn off the light, Koala!

AAAI

1. Find the words and circle them.

a	d	w	o	g	h	o	s	t	k	x	f	s
j	h	n	k	a	n	b	j	v	w	v	b	k
t	r	i	c	k	o	r	t	r	e	a	t	e
l	c	g	c	s	t	o	y	s	p	m	i	l
z	e	h	o	b	a	b	a	t	d	p	m	e
w	i	t	c	h	i	v	a	d	f	i	k	t
q	v	o	w	l	m	h	r	e	b	r	n	o
t	j	a	c	k	o	l	a	n	t	e	r	n

Suche die Wörter senkrecht und waagrecht. Kreise sie ein.

> **night   witch   ghost   Trick or Treat**
> **vampire   skeleton   bat   Jack O'Lantern**

2. Fill in the missing words.

It's Halloween. It's a dark _____.

The candles are shining in the _____.

A _____ is crossing the street.

A _____ is flying around.

A _____ is hiding behind a bush.

A _____ is clattering with its bones.

A _____ is shouting "Boo!"

The creatures meet in front of a house and ring the bell.

The door opens and they shout out loud: "_____!"

1₂³3. Number the speech bubbles in the correct order.

Turn off the light, Koala! ◯

I have an idea! ◯

Nobody will be scared of you in a vampire costume. ◯

I don't know. Let's go and try some costumes. ◯

But what's that, Sally, where's your costume? ◯

Streiche die falsche Ergänzung durch.

4. Cross out.

Koala wants to be a vampire / a Jack O'Lantern.

Sally likes / doesn't like the bat costume.

Koala has to turn off the light to see Sally's skeleton costume / ghost costume.

Sally and Koala are trying some costumes at home / in a shop.

What would you like to be at Halloween?

I would like to be a _____.

📕 Comic

A surprise for Father Christmas

1. What can you see on the Christmas branch? Look, write and draw.

Schreibe die Wörter anhand der Tabelle. Male die letzten beiden Bilder selbst.

1 = a	5 = e	9 = i	13 = n	17 = s
2 = b	6 = f	10 = k	14 = o	18 = t
3 = c	7 = g	11 = l	15 = p	
4 = d	8 = h	12 = m	16 = r	

① _ _ _ _ _ _
  3 1 13 4 11 5

② _ _ _ _ _ _   _ _ _ _ _ _ _ _ _
  6 1 18 8 5 16   3 8 16 9 17 18 12 1 17

③ _ _ _ _ _ _ _
  15 16 5 17 5 13 18

④ _ _ _ _ _ _ _
  17 18 14 3 10 9 13 7

⑤ _ _ _ _ _
  1 13 7 5 11

⑥ _ _ _ _
  2 5 11 11

⑦ _ _ _ _
  17 18 1 16

 2. Correct or wrong? Circle the correct letter and find the word.

	correct	wrong
The milk and biscuits are for Father Christmas.	B	S
There are toys on the Christmas tree.	T	E
Father Christmas comes in a helicopter.	A	L
The presents are in a sack.	L	R

The word is: _ _ _ _

3. Read the comic again and fill in the missing words.

People have a Christmas tree with _ _ _ _ _, _ _ _ _ _ _ _ _ and
_ _ _ _ _ and an _ _ _ _ _ on top.

Who brings the _ _ _ _ _ _ _ _? Father Christmas.

He comes on a _ _ _ _ _ _ pulled by nine _ _ _ _ _ _ _ _ _.

Father Christmas comes down the _ _ _ _ _ _ _ _.

He says:

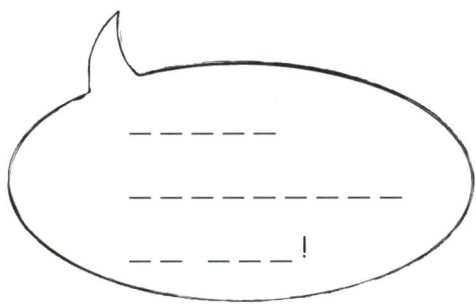

Look at the comics again. Find the missing words and write them into the squares. The letters in the marked squares form a sentence.

Comic 1: We had a great ☐☐☐☐ at the beach. 1

Comic 2: Who's ☐☐☐☐☐☐☐☐ there? 2

Comic 3: The ☐☐☐☐☐ is for the living room. 3

Comic 4: I'd like the carrot soup – and a ham ☐☐☐☐☐☐☐☐ , please. 4

Comic 5: It's ☐☐☐☐☐☐ today. 5

Comic 6: No thanks, I prefer ☐☐☐☐☐☐☐☐ . 6

Comic 7: Oh no, the ☐☐☐☐☐☐☐ skates are too big. 7

Comic 8: Walk ☐☐☐☐☐☐☐☐ on to the ferry wharf. 8

Comic 9: This is Sila, the ☐☐☐☐☐☐ . 9

Comic 10: Have you got a ☐☐☐☐☐☐☐☐ or a stomachache? 10

Comic 11: Help me in the ☐☐☐☐☐☐☐☐ , please. 11

Comic 12: I'm Jorgos from ☐☐☐☐☐☐☐ . 12

Comic 13: I'd like to see the Statue of ☐☐☐☐☐☐☐☐ . 13

Comic 14: I'm a wicked ☐☐☐☐☐ . 14

Comic 15: Father ☐☐☐☐☐☐☐☐☐ is coming 15

down the ☐☐☐☐☐☐ . 16

Trage die fehlenden Wörter in die Kästchen ein. Die Buchstaben in den markierten Feldern ergeben einen Satz.

‾ ‾ ‾ ‾
1 2 3 4

‾ ‾ ‾ ‾ ‾
5 6 7 8 9

‾ ‾ ‾ ‾ ‾ ‾ ‾.
10 11 12 13 14 15 16